For Aunt Snep - Ch.P.

Want to know
lots to do

A Day at the Museum

Florence Ducatteau & Chantal Peten

Clavis

So, this is a museum! Museums are buildings
in which objects of historical, scientific, artistic,
or cultural importance are stored and exhibited.
Most museums are large with many rooms and
halls. There are many different types of museums,
including historical museums, scientific museums,
natural history museums, car museums, and art
museums. Grandma and Grandpa have brought
Claire and Billy to a fine arts museum—
it mostly stores and exhibits paintings, statues,
and sculptures.

The main hall of the museum

Claire, Billy, Grandma, and Grandpa are standing at the ticket and information desk in the main hall. Grandpa buys four tickets. They will visit the museum's "permanent collection," the most important collection of the artwork the museum has that is on display—*exhibited*—all year long.

Throughout the main hall, members of the museum staff help visitors find what they're looking for—a specific painting, a cafeteria, the movie room, or the restroom. Some staff members guard the museum, making sure visitors don't do anything they're not supposed to do, like touch fragile objects, damage anything, or steal the works of art.

EXHIBIT

Did you know that some museums are free?

How can you visit the museum?

You can visit a museum on your own, with your family, with your friends, or with your class from school. You can also be taken around by a museum guide on a tour of the museum; that's a good way to find out more about all the things you're seeing.

On the left there's a museum volunteer in a flowered hat. She has organized some activities for a group of children—today she's asking the children to find all the hats in the paintings in this room.

On the right you can see a tour guide leading a group of visitors around the rooms. She's giving them explanations about the museum and what they're seeing in each exhibit.

Sometimes you can get an audio guided tour at the museum. Then you can listen through headphones to a spoken explanation of everything there is to see.

Did you know
that a "catalog" is a book about
the museum, an exhibit, or an artist whose
work is exhibited at the museum?

How does an exhibit get made?

In toy museums, very old toys and more modern toys are out on exhibit. In a historical museum you'll see paintings or photographs showing how people lived a long time ago, the clothes people wore, and the tools and implements they used. In a car museum you'll see the very first cars ever made a long time ago, racing cars, and modern electric cars. And in a museum of fine arts, like the one Claire and Billy are in, you'll see works of art displayed on the walls, on the floor, and on pedestals.

There are informational signs next to every object on display, explaining what the object is, what it's for, how old it is, and where it's from. The informational signs next to works of art give the title of the painting or sculpture, the name of the artist, when it was made, and the materials it's made from.

Did you know that some objects in a museum are worth a lot of money and therefore attract thieves?

The art thief who nearly got away!

Behind the scenes

Visitors can walk through most of the rooms in a museum, but not all. Visitors cannot enter the rooms in which art restorers are mending, or restoring, damaged works of art. Restoring art is a very precise job that takes a lot of time and concentration. When art restoration is done well, you can't tell that the piece was ever damaged.

The museum director—the "curator"—purchases pieces of art for the museum to add to the museum's permanent collection. The curator's responsible for keeping the pieces safe, determines how they will be displayed, and creates events to bring in visitors to see the exhibits. When a new piece of art arrives at the museum, the restorers and the museum staff carefully unwrap it under the watchful eye of the curator. It absolutely must not be damaged! Then the piece is usually stored for a little while before it is put on exhibit.

Did you know that there are works of art that you can't exhibit? You can't exhibit a dance performance or a theatrical performance, for instance. To see these performances after they're over, photographs or films taken of the performances are put on display.

The museum on the inside

This is what Claire and Billy's Museum of Fine Arts looks like on the inside. On either side of the entrance hall there are elevators and stairs leading to the other floors.

Grandma and Grandpa have taken Claire and Billy to the exhibit of paintings, sculptures, and statues from the 19th Century. Claire and Billy especially like the sculptures. There are some made out of plaster, stone, and marble, as well as some of metal and bronze. Claire imitates the sculpture called *Crazy violence* by the Belgian artist, Rik Wouters. Billy has sat down on Spanish artist, Pablo Picasso's *She Goat*. This is against the rules and the angry guard says Billy has to get up immediately. Oops!

In the rooms and halls displaying old paintings and sculptures, all the artwork is over 100 years ago and the artists died a long time ago. In the room and halls displaying modern and contemporary artwork, all the artwork was created less than 100 years ago and many of the artists are still alive.

The museum on the outside

This is what Claire and Billy's Museum of Fine Arts looks like from the outside. It is a big, old building with a glass dome. Each room and hall in the museum displays beautiful, world-famous collections of artwork.

The curator organizes smaller exhibits of modern art. These exhibits sometimes last only a few months and then get packed up and travel to museums in different cities and even different countries.
This is how people from all over the world can see the same exhibits.

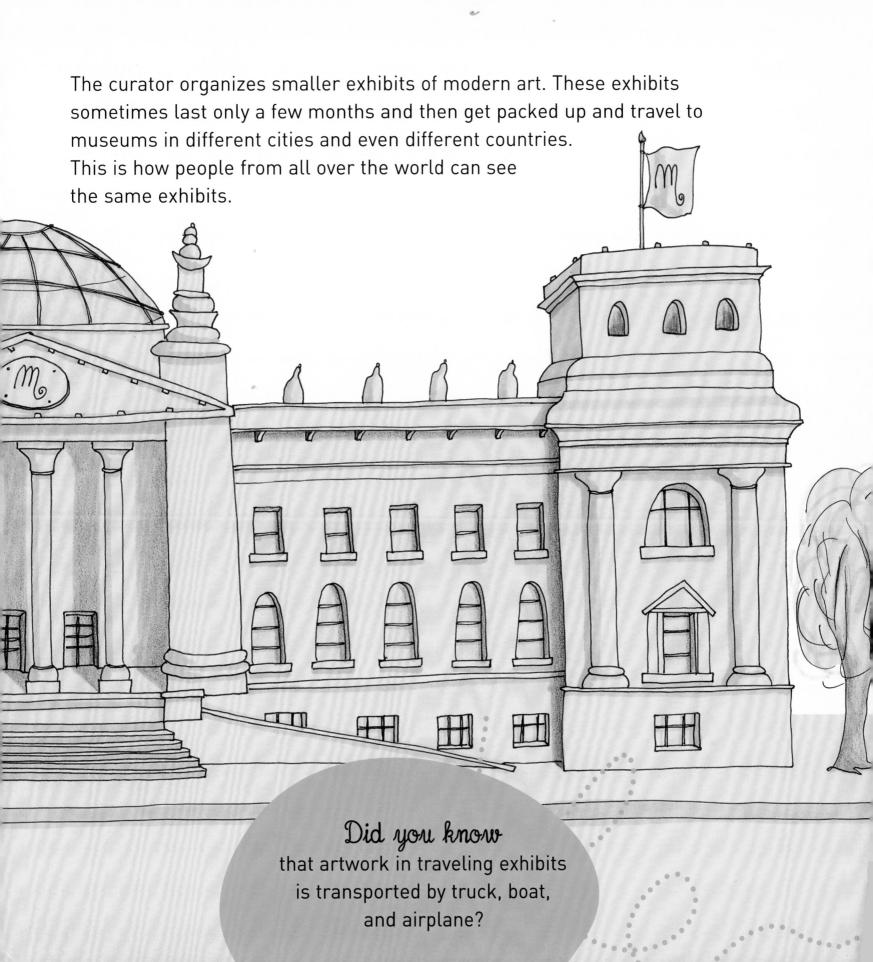

Did you know
that artwork in traveling exhibits is transported by truck, boat, and airplane?

In a tower on the far side of the museum, there's a temporary exhibit of the work of the Swiss artist, Alberto Giacometti. His paintings and sculptures are on display and there's a short video about his life. In the tower on the opposite side of the museum is a big movie theater where you can see movies about art and artists.

Sometimes a room or hall is named after a famous artist who has a lot of artwork in the museum. Only his or her artwork is on display in that room or hall.

The curator's office is above the museum shop. Some large museums have more than one curator.

The museum has a cafeteria-style restaurant right under the glass dome.

In the museum's basement you will find the restorers' studios and the warehouse where artwork is stored. Next to that is the lounge and locker room for the museum staff, guards, and other people who work in the museum.

When you're not looking at art in the museum

On your left you will see the museum shop. Here you can buy catalogs, postcards, gifts, and all sorts of things on which artwork is portrayed: posters, T-shirts, jewelry, tote bags, and so on. Claire and Billy each buy a postcard of their favorite piece of art and Grandpa buys them the museum catalog. They'll plan to take these to school for show-and-tell.

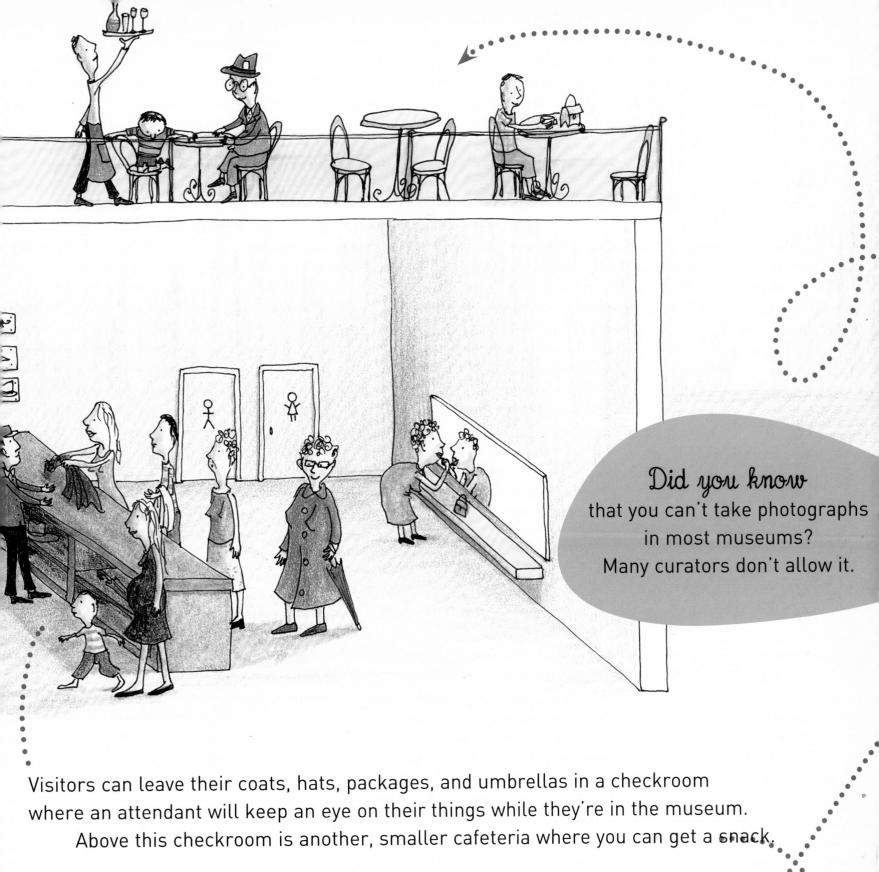

Did you know
that you can't take photographs
in most museums?
Many curators don't allow it.

Visitors can leave their coats, hats, packages, and umbrellas in a checkroom
where an attendant will keep an eye on their things while they're in the museum.
Above this checkroom is another, smaller cafeteria where you can get a snack.

Types of museums

Claire and Billy are standing in front of the Air and Space Museum. This is a science and technology museum where you can learn about all kinds of airplanes, space rockets, and the solar system.

The Natural History Museum is also a scientific museum, but everything on display here has to do with nature—mammals, reptiles, birds, fish, plants, the ocean, and rocks and minerals. Claire and Billy always go to their favorite room first—
the hall of dinosaurs!

This is the Guggenheim Museum in New York City. It is filled with modern art. The building itself is a work of art, designed like a gigantic modern sculpture by the architect Frank Lloyd Wright.

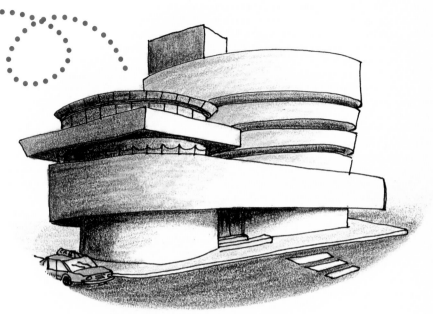

Did you know that people want to see many different things and there's probably a museum for everything they're interested in?

Claire and Billy are next to a museum that's housed in a huge ship called an aircraft carrier. Here you can find out about the history, building, sailing, and use of boats and ships. You can also learn how sailors and captains live aboard different boats and ships.

My own museum

This big pink box is like my own museum, you see—
with collections of this and that, all to exhibit *me*:
My first shoes, an old stuffed rabbit, tickets to shows;
a bracelet, a doll, and loads of old photos.

This box holds my most pretty poems and drawings,
report cards, hair from my first haircut, and homemade things;
all my baby teeth are in this small box with a fairy, you see—
come a little closer and take a guided tour with me!

Step right up to my museum of everything!
This box is filled to the brim with race cars, balls, and some string;
a paper hat, my favorite planes, some menus, and a flag;
a love letter, a mitt, and a stuffed animal with one leg.

I keep everything, even the junk—I like to hang onto it all.
I push and shove until there's room for one more something small.
You say I need a second museum? You're probably right, and so—
I'll just keep collecting things. When my exhibit's ready, I'll let you know!

Do you want to make your own museum?
Do you want to bet that yours will also be filled to the brim?

Framing your own artwork

You can make frames for your own works of art. Ask for some help from an adult or older person.

1. Pick a drawing, painting, or photograph and position it in the middle of a thick piece of 8-1/2" x 11" cardboard, which will become your frame.

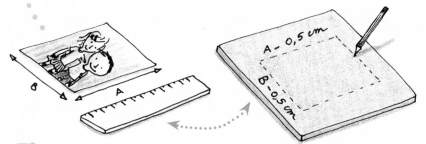

2. With a pencil, draw the outline of the art on the cardboard, making sure the outline is ½" shorter and ½" narrower than the art itself (that way you won't see the edges of your art in the frame).

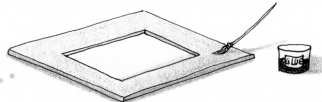

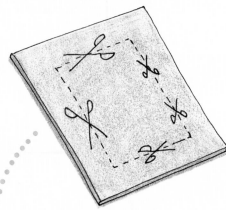

3. With an adult's help, use strong scissors to carefully cut out the inside of your frame along the lines.

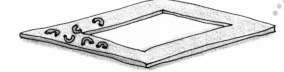

4. Decorate the frame any way you like: Use paint, glue shells or dry pasta to it, or make a collage on it. You're the artist, so just use your imagination!

5. Position your artwork so it shows through the frame. Tape it to the back of the frame. You can add an adhesive hook to the back of the frame if you want to hang the frame, or attach a foot if you want the frame to stand on a table. All done!

All those sculptures!

Take a close look at the sculptures.
Now cover up the page with a piece of paper
so you can't see the sculptures anymore and
open the flap.

See the shadows of the sculptures?
Which two shadows are missing? Do you
know which shadow belongs with which
sculpture? Uncover the sculptures to see
if you were right.